WORLD IN  FORESTS

Steve Pollock

Illustrated by Peter Wingham

Belitha Press

First published in Great Britain in 1990 by
Belitha Press Limited
31 Newington Green, London N16 9PU

Text copyright © Steve Pollock 1990
Illustrations copyright © Peter Wingham 1990
Editor: Neil Champion

All rights reserved. No part of this book may be reproduced or utilised in any form or by any means, electronic or mechanical, including photocopying, recording or by any information storage and retrieval system, without permission in writing from the publisher.

ISBN 1-85561-006-X (hardback)
ISBN 1-85561-026-4 (paperback)

Printed in the UK by MacLehose For Imago Publishing
Printed on recycled paper (135 gsm Envirocote)

Contents

What is a forest?	4
Where are the forests?	6
The life of a tree	8
How trees help us	10
Vanishing forests	12
Your tropical forests	14
Cutting down the trees	16
What happens after?	18
Managing the forests	20
Who took the trees?	22
Saving the trees	24
You can help	26
Forests fact file	28
Further information	30
Glossary	31
Index	32

What is a forest?

A forest is a large, wild place full of trees and the plants and animals that live among them.

The way you think about a forest will depend upon what kind of forest it is, where in the world you live and also the time of year. Some forests are light and airy places; others are dark and scary.

Forests take a long time to grow. They grow when land is left alone for a long time. They will even take over your back garden if you don't watch out!

A forest has many layers. The top layer is where the leaves of the tallest trees catch the sunlight. Trees need energy from sunlight to help them grow.

Underneath this layer (called the **canopy**), the forest is shady. This is where you see the **trunks** of the trees and other small trees and bushes.

The next is called the shrub layer. Plants and herbs grow here. Forest animals that live on the ground can be found.

Underneath those plants and shrubs are the mosses that make up the ground layer.

Where are the forests?

A map of the world showing the main forest zones.

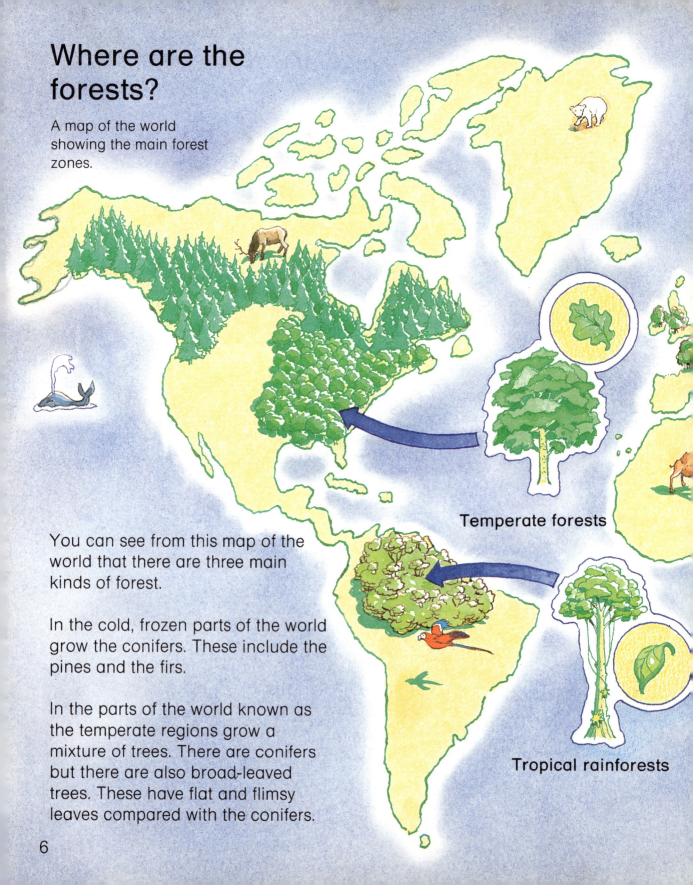

Temperate forests

Tropical rainforests

You can see from this map of the world that there are three main kinds of forest.

In the cold, frozen parts of the world grow the conifers. These include the pines and the firs.

In the parts of the world known as the temperate regions grow a mixture of trees. There are conifers but there are also broad-leaved trees. These have flat and flimsy leaves compared with the conifers.

Coniferous forests

Conifer leaf

Temperate leaf

Rainforest leaf

In the warmest part of the world around the **equator** grow the **tropical** forests. These trees have leaves like broad-leaved trees. These forests are very important to all on Earth.

The life of a tree

A tree has a trunk, branches and leaves. It has **roots** and they grow underground. The roots feed the tree with water and goodness taken from the soil. Leaves catch the sunlight. This also gives the tree energy.

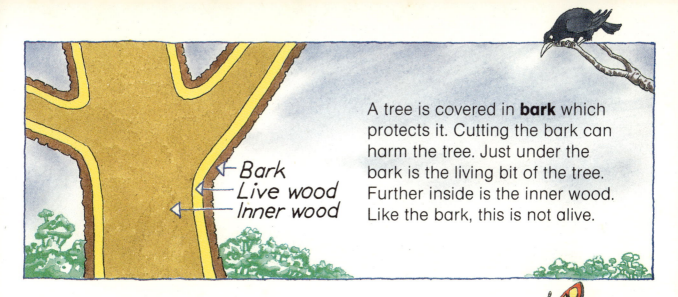

A tree is covered in **bark** which protects it. Cutting the bark can harm the tree. Just under the bark is the living bit of the tree. Further inside is the inner wood. Like the bark, this is not alive.

Bark
Live wood
Inner wood

The tree gets thicker each year as it grows. It leaves a ring of wood for each year it has been alive. If you count all the rings in the trunk of a tree that has been cut down, you can tell how old it is.

The Bristle cone pine is the oldest living thing on Earth. It can live to be over 4,000 years old. A tree this old would have been a **sapling** when the Great Pyramids or Stonehenge were built.

How trees help us

Falling rain water is absorbed by trees and plants and soil.

In tropical countries there is a very wet time of year called the rainy season. Rain pours down and water goes everywhere. The forest can soak up the water like a sponge, holding onto it for a very long time.

Without the trees and plants the rain water washes away the soil causing floods.

When a forest is cut down, there is nothing to catch all this water. When this happens there can be so much water about that it causes flooding. Floods can wash away soil, buildings and even people.

All over the world forests are supplying us with oxygen. All plants make oxygen from sunlight. This is called **photosynthesis**. Each time a forest is cut down, we slowly cut off our oxygen supply.

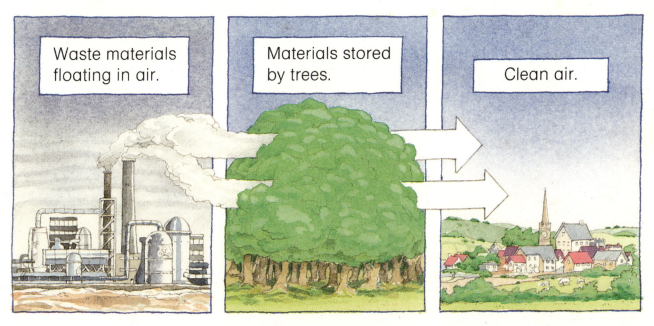

Forests help the air we breathe stay clean. Some factories produce small amounts of waste materials which escape into the air and float around. When they come to a forest, the trees can use and store them, keeping the air clean. If forests are destroyed, the air becomes dirtier.

Vanishing forests

Trees and forests are important to us and yet tropical forests all over the world are being cut down all the time. Every minute 100 acres of tropical forest is damaged or destroyed altogether. Every year an area the size of England, Scotland and Wales is cut down. Why does this happen? People clear the forests so they can sell the wood from the trees. Some wood is very valuable (for example, **teak** and **mahogany**). The rest is cut up into chippings. It is then used to produce chipboard.

When all the forest has been cleared grass is grown in the soil left behind. Cattle feed on the grass and are sold to rich countries. The cattle are turned into hamburgers. It's not just trees that go when the forest goes. What do you think happens to the animals? Where do the people who live in the forest go?

Tropical forests have more variety of plants and animals than anywhere else on Earth. Some are useful. The Madagascar periwinkle, a plant, has chemicals in it which can help save the lives of people with **leukaemia**. There must be plants and animals not yet discovered that could help us in lots of different ways. Each half hour one more plant or animal as yet undiscovered becomes **extinct**.

The forest is home to tribal indians. They have lived in balance with the forest using what they need to live there without destroying it. Now with modern machinery and the need to make money quickly, people are destroying the indians' homes. Where can they go? They cannot change easily to a modern way of life. They catch diseases and die. Sometimes they are driven from the forest by force and are killed.

Your tropical forests

Look carefully in this room. Some of the things in this room would not be there if it were not for tropical forests. Can you work out what things come from tropical forests?

There is a mahogany table. Mahogany is a precious hardwood. It is used to make expensive furniture.

Many house plants come from tropical forests. They can also be grown in greenhouses and cultivated.

Fruit – bananas, mangos, avocados – come from tropical forests.

Rattan furniture is made from the rattan plant. It is grown by people who make it into furniture and sell it.

Tropical fish live in the rivers which flow through tropical forests. People now breed many kinds in fish tanks all over the world.

This amazon parrot is kept as a pet. They cannot be bred in captivity. Parrots are taken from the forests where they live.

15

Cutting down the trees

In a tropical forest the soil is very thin and sandy. Tropical trees take up the goodness from the soil very quickly. So the soil is never thick and brown. People cut down the trees so they can grow crops. As the crops grow, they take out goodness in the soil. Two or three years later there is no goodness left in the soil. Nothing more will grow. People move on and cut down more forest. Water from the heavy tropical rains washes the soil away.

There is nothing to hold the soil there. It washes away into the rivers. The hot tropical sun turns the bare ground hard as rock. Nobody can dig the soil. No seed can grow there. Nothing can live there now. Where once huge trees grew, there is now only dry, hard and useless land.

What happens after?

Pulling down forests can lead to **drought** and **starvation**. That means there are not enough trees left to hold onto water, to keep the soil from blowing away or to provide firewood for the people to burn. In Ethiopia most of the forests have been removed. There is no doubt that the lack of trees made the drought in Ethiopia much worse.

Without forests life would be different. We can never be really sure how life will change but we know some of the risks. Let's look at what might happen if we keep destroying the forests.

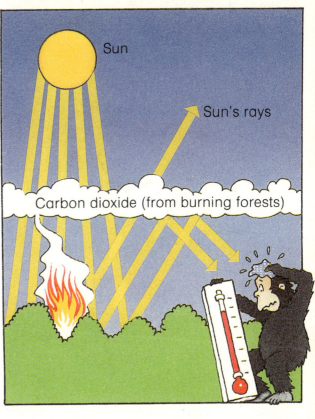

Tropical forests are often burned. When this happens a gas called **carbon dioxide** is released into the air. As more forests are burned more carbon dioxide is released. Too much carbon dioxide in the air stops heat from the Earth escaping into space. This means the Earth will get warmer. The world's weather may change causing problems such as a rise in the level of the oceans. This is called the **greenhouse effect**.

Destroying forests does not just affect the people who live nearby, it affects everyone. Tropical forests help keep the world's climate in balance.

Managing the forests

Over 100 years ago, in the USA people realised that forests were being destroyed. Something had to be done otherwise there would be no wild places left. In 1872 the first National Park, Yellowstone, was created. In a national park forests could never be cut down but were kept for the good of everyone in the country. Stopping people cutting down forests is not the only way to help forests survive. It is possible to use them wisely by managing them properly. Some trees are called hardwoods and they can keep growing even if the trunk is cut. Trees like this can be **coppiced**.

Tree coppicing

Of course not all trees grow like hardwoods. The pines and firs are softwoods. They never can grow again once they have been cut down. In parts of Europe and America they are grown on **plantations**. When they are at the right size they are cut down and used to make furniture and woodpulp. Woodpulp is used to make paper so many plantations are cut down to supply the world with paper. When one plantation is cleared young trees are planted to grow more softwood. By carefully managing the forests, it is possible to use them and save them.

Who took the trees?

Five thousand years ago nearly all of Britain was covered in forest. A squirrel travelling the length of Britain could have moved the whole distance along the branches of trees. It would never have needed to come down to the ground. Today that would be impossible. Most of Britain's forest has gone.

Most of Europe has a similar history. The reason is that humans began cutting down the forest to help them live. They would cut down the trees to make space for fields to grow their crops and keep their domestic animals.

They would use the wood to make houses to live in. Wood was also needed to burn as fuel. Fire was necessary to keep people warm and to cook their food. As people became more skilful in making tools and weapons, charcoal was used as a fuel to make iron.

Charcoal was made in earth ovens, which kept out the air. Charcoal is

wood that has been burnt very slowly and then can be burnt again. Whole forests were cut down for charcoal.

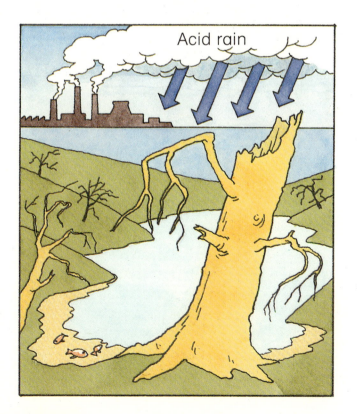

In North America the destruction of forests took a much shorter time. Only a matter of three hundred years. This was because so many people colonised North America so quickly.

Many people all over the world now realise that forests need to be saved and are working hard to stop them being destroyed. Yet it is not just cutting them down which can kill a forest. Chemicals put into the air by industrial processes turn rain slightly acid. When this **acid rain** keeps falling on some forests the trees may die. Sometimes nature rather than people can cause the destruction. Dutch elm disease killed many of Britain's elm trees during the 1970s. A fungus spread by beetles grew in the tree eventually killing it. Nearly all of the elm trees were wiped out.

Saving the trees

In a village in India women had to walk a long way to get firewood from the forest. They burnt firewood for cooking their food. One day men came with axes to chop the forest down and sell the trees. The women were angry because they would have no more firewood and would have to walk even further to find some. So each of the women hugged a tree. The men could not cut down the trees with the women in the way. Each time the men came to cut down the forest the women would run and hug the trees to save them. In the end the forest was saved. It took the brave village women to make sure their precious forest lived on.

In Costa Rica, in Central America, there is an area of land which will become a tropical forest and a national park. The idea is to gather enough money to grow a forest using seedlings from a particular kind of tree. In twenty years, a complete forest will have been grown

in which many different plants and animals will be able to live and thrive.

Rather than cut down more tropical forest new fast growing trees are being planted on land where forests used to grow. One fast growing tree is an Acacia from Australia. After three years it is ten metres tall. It can be harvested after 15 years when its diameter is 60 cm. Native trees in the rainforest take up to 50 years to reach the same size. Conifers take 80 years and broad-leaved trees take 200 years!

You can help

Bark rubbing

Tree planting

A forest is an exciting place to explore. Make sure you go into a forest with someone who knows it well. It is easy to get lost in a forest.

Do conifers, broad-leaved or tropical trees grow there? Have a look at the leaves to find out. Are the trees nearly all the same kind? If so, what are they called?

Keeping a field notebook

Making a bark rubbing of a tree is a fun way to keep a record of what a tree is like. Do rubbings of different kinds of tree trunks. Can you tell the difference between some trees? You should also keep a notebook to record the discoveries you make in your forest.

No matter what forest you are in changes will take place. Visit the forest and collect different parts of trees. You can choose a special tree. Measure how wide it is. Make friends with it.

Forests Fact File

Disappearing rainforests

Every year, an area of tropical rainforest equal to the size of Great Britain is destroyed. This means that within one minute (the time it takes for you to read this page, for instance) another 100 acres of rainforest will have disappeared for ever. It has taken over 100 million years for the complicated and fragile rainforest environment to evolve. Now in less than a person's lifetime it could almost all be destroyed.

Solving the problems?

Rainforests are important to the people who live in them. They provide shelter, food, clothing, medicine and pleasure. They are also vitally important to the well being of the rest of life on Earth. They help keep our air clean and provide us with oxygen. They are the richest source of different types of plant and animal life on Earth. This means that they could give us new sources of food and medicines which at the moment we know nothing about. They need saving. Today many people around the world are campaigning to do just this.

Food facts

Coffee, tea, sugar, bananas, pineapples, oranges, lemons, avocados, rice, maize, cocoa (the plant we get chocolate from), and peanuts are just some of the foods that originally came from the rainforests. Today, many of these foods are grown outside the forests. There may be over 1,500 tropical plants that people could cultivate and use as vegetables but which have never really been thought about. We are in danger of losing valuable plants such as these for ever.

Disappearing species

We know that there are about 1.5 million different kinds of plants and animals. Some people think that in the rainforests live another 30 million kinds that as yet we know nothing about. We may never find out anything about them. Why? Because each day another fifty kinds disappear for ever as their rainforest homes are cut down.

Empty forests?

Before the Europeans arrived and started to exploit the rainforests, tribal indians lived in harmony with their very special and fragile environment. They did not cut down vast areas to use the wood from the trees and grow crops and feed animals. They used the forest's resources carefully which meant that the forest would always be there. Today all this has changed. Their way of life is under threat because the forests on which they depend are being destroyed at a great rate. By 1980, about 40% of the total of the Earth's surface covered in rainforest, had been stripped of its trees. In Brazil (a country in South America, where Europeans arrived in the fifteenth century) there were about 5 million forest indians in 1500. Today there is less than 5% (some 200,000)

They have been killed with guns and diseases brought by the white people and they have in many instances been driven off their lands by greedy people.

Did you know?

Plants and trees in the rainforests have provided us with lots of special chemicals used in helping to fight disease. One out of every four chemicals or medicines in the high street chemist, for instance, originally came from the rainforests. Tribal indians living in the forests have long known the special qualities of the trees and plants that grow around them. One such tribe in South America grows 21 different types of plant to use as medicines. They grow another 27 types which they use for producing different coloured dyes to paint their bodies and colour their clothes with.

Further information

There are many organisations involved with helping nature and our environment. Below are the addresses of just some of the more well known ones that you may like to contact. They may also be able to put you in touch with local organisations, if you want to get actively involved with things such as fund-raising through sponsored events. Remember, our natural world needs every friend and helper it can get!

Friends of the Earth
26-28 Underwood Street
London N1 7JQ

World Wide Fund for Nature
Panda House
Weyside Park
Godalming
Surrey GU7 1XR

Greenpeace
30-31 Islington Green
London N1 8XT

Fauna and Flora Preservation Society
79-83 North Street
Brighton
East Sussex BN1 1ZA

The Conservation Trust
George Palmer Site
Northumberland Avenue
Reading
Berkshire RG2 7PW

Royal Society for the Protection of Birds
The Lodge
Sandy
Bedfordshire

The People's Trust for Endangered Species
Hamble house
Meadrow
Godalming
Surrey GU7 3JX

Glossary

Acid rain Rain that is mixed with polluting chemicals. It makes a weak acid and is very harmful to trees.

Bark The outer protecting layer of a tree.

Canopy The topmost layer of leaves and branches in a forest.

Carbon dioxide A colourless and non-smelling gas which is in the air around us.

Conifers Trees that have cones. They often keep their leaves all year round.

Coppiced Trees that have been cut and trimmed which then grow from many trunks rather than from one.

Drought A lack of water. In some areas and countries of the world this can lead to very bad conditions for people, animals and vegetation.

Equator An imaginary line that runs around the middle of the Earth, passing through the hottest and wettest regions.

Extinct Something that does not exist anymore. The dinosaurs, for example, are extinct.

Greenhouse effect The warming up of the Earth due to the blanketing effect of man-made carbon dioxide in the air.

Leukaemia Cancer of the blood. It is a disease that can kill people.

Oxygen A gas without taste, colour or smell. It is very important to all living things and is found in the air we breathe.

Photosynthesis The means by which plants turn energy from sunlight into food for them to grow and reproduce.

Plantations An estate designed to produce things, such as cotton, rubber, tea and sugar, on a large scale.

Sapling A young tree.

Tropical Something which comes from a region of the Earth known as the tropics. These run on either side of the equator, and in terms of climate, are very hot and generally very wet.

Trunk The stem of a tree; usually its thickest part.

31

Index

Acacia 25
Acid rain 23
Air 11, 19, 22
Animals 5, 12, 13, 22, 23, 25
Australia 25

Bark 9, 27
Branches 8, 22
Bristle cone pine 9
Britain 22
Broad-leaved trees 6, 7, 25, 26
Bushes 5

Canopy 5
Carbon dioxide 19
Cattle 12
Charcoal 22
Chemicals 13, 23
Climate 19
Conifers 6, 25, 26
Coppiced 20
Costa Rica 24
Crops 17, 22

Disease 13
Drought 18
Dutch Elm disease 23

Earth 7, 13, 19
Energy 5, 8
Equator 7
Ethiopia 18
Europe 21, 22
Extinct 13

Factories 11
Firewood 18, 22, 24
Firs 6, 21
Fish (tropical) 15
floods 10
Forest 4, 5, 6, 7, 10, 11, 12, 13, 14, 15, 17, 18, 19, 20, 22, 23, 24, 25, 26, 27
Fruit (tropical) 15
Fuel 22
Furniture 21

Greenhouse effect 19

Hamburgers 12
Herbs 22
Houses 22

India 24

Leaves 5, 6, 8, 26
Leukaemia 13

Madagascar periwinkle 13
Mahogany 12, 15

National Parks 20, 24

Oceans 19
Oxygen 11

Paper 21
Photosynthesis 11
Pines 6, 21
Plantations 21
Plants 5, 10, 11, 13, 25
Plants (tropical) 15

Rainwater 10, 17, 23
Rainy season 10
Rivers 17
Roots 8

Sapling 9
Shrub 5
Soil 10, 17, 18
Starvation 17
Sun 17
Sunlight 5, 8, 11

Teak 12
Temperate regions 6
Trees 5, 6, 7, 8, 9, 10, 11, 12, 17, 18, 20, 21, 22, 23, 24, 25, 26, 27
Tribal indians 13
Tropical rainforests 7, 10, 12, 13, 14, 17, 19, 24, 25, 26
Trunk 5, 8, 27

USA 20, 21, 23

Waste 11
Water 8, 10, 17, 18
Weather 19
Wood 9, 22, 23
Woodpulp 21

Yellowstone National Park (USA) 20